OUR NATIONAL PARKS

# Yosemite
# Sequoia and Kings Canyon
# Hawaii

*by Frances Wood*

*Illustrated with photographs in color*

FOLLETT PUBLISHING COMPANY    CHICAGO

123456789

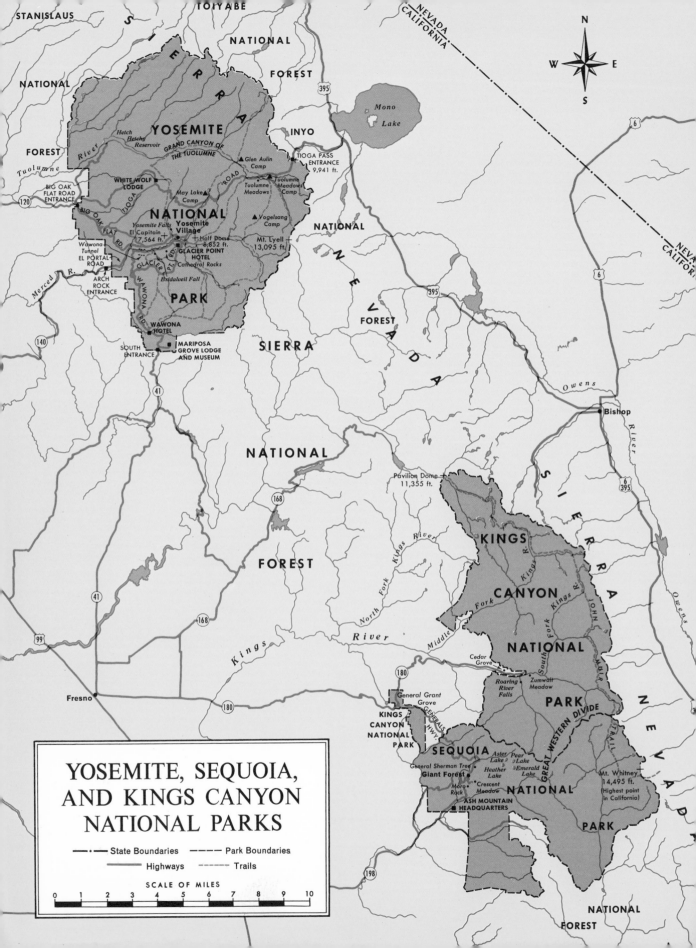

STANISLAUS

TOIYABE

NEVADA
CALIFORNIA

N
W    E
S

NATIONAL

NATIONAL

FOREST

SIERRA

FOREST

120

YOSEMITE

Tuolumne    River

Hetch Hetchy Reservoir

GRAND CANYON OF THE TUOLUMNE

▲ Glen Aulin Camp

WHITE WOLF LODGE

May Lake Camp ▲

TIOGA    ROAD

Tuolumne Meadows

▲ Tuolumne Meadows Camp

TIOGA PASS ENTRANCE 9,941 ft.

INYO

NATIONAL

BIG OAK FLAT ROAD ENTRANCE

BIG OAK    FLAT    RD.

NATIONAL

Yosemite Falls
El Capitan 7,564 ft. ✛
Yosemite Village

✛ Half Dome 8,852 ft.

▲ Vogelsang Camp

✛ Mt. Lyell 13,095 ft.

FOREST

Wawona Tunnel
EL PORTAL ROAD

GLACIER POINT HOTEL
Cathedral Rocks

GLACIER    PT. RD.

PARK

Mono Lake

6

Merced R.

ARCH ROCK ENTRANCE

Bridalveil Fall

WAWONA    RD.

140

WAWONA HOTEL

SOUTH ENTRANCE

MARIPOSA GROVE LODGE AND MUSEUM

SIERRA

395

Owens

6

41

NATIONAL

Bishop ●

River

NATIONAL

168

Pavilion Dome 11,355 ft.

SIERRA

6
395

FOREST

North    fork    Kings    River

KINGS

CANYON

41

168

Kings

River

Middle

South    fork    Kings    R.

JOHN    MUIR    TRAIL

NATIONAL

99

180

Fresno ●

180

Cedar Grove

Roaring River Falls
Zumwalt Meadow

PARK

GREAT WESTERN DIVIDE

Owens

General Grant Grove

KINGS CANYON NATIONAL PARK

GENERALS    HWY.

SEQUOIA

General Sherman Tree
Giant Forest

Aster Lake ○
Heather Lake

Pear Lake
Emerald Lake

Mt. Whitney 14,495 ft. (Highest point in California)

Moro Rock ▲
Crescent Meadow

ASH MOUNTAIN HEADQUARTERS

NATIONAL

PARK

198

NATIONAL

FOREST

# YOSEMITE, SEQUOIA, AND KINGS CANYON NATIONAL PARKS

— · — · —  State Boundaries      — — — —  Park Boundaries
————————  Highways              - - - - - -  Trails

SCALE OF MILES

0   1   2   3   4   5   6   7   8   9   10

# Sequoia and Kings Canyon National Park

These parks preserve the largest, and some of the oldest, living trees in the world. They are the giant sequoias, often called the "Big Trees."

Sequoia and Kings Canyon national parks lie along the west side of the great mountain chain known as the Sierra Nevada, in central California. In addition to the Big Trees, the parks contain some of the highest mountains and deepest canyons in North America.

The two parks are close together, and the same superintendent and park rangers manage both of them. They are connected by a wide and beautiful road, the Generals Highway.

3

*The Parker Group of giant sequoias in Giant Forest.*

4

The Sequoia and Kings Canyon parks contain many Big Trees whose trunks are twenty feet or more in diameter. The largest sequoia of all is the General Sherman Tree, which stands in the Giant Forest in Sequoia National Park.

This tree is believed to be the largest living thing in the world. It is 272 feet tall, and its trunk, at the base, has a diameter of 36.5 feet.

It would take more than twenty children, with outstretched arms, to circle the trunk, which is wider than many city streets. Forty houses could be built from the wood in it.

The General Grant Tree, in Kings Canyon National Park, is the second-largest sequoia. It is 267 feet tall and has a diameter of 40.3 feet.

These two great trees, and many other sequoias, are thought to be 3,000 to 4,000 years old. And they are still growing and producing seeds. So no one knows how many more hundreds or thousands of years they may continue to grow.

Giant sequoias are native only in the Sierra Nevada, and are found at altitudes of 4,000 to 8,000 feet. They usually grow among other trees, such as firs and the tall sugar pine and lovely incense cedars.

The young sequoia is shaped like a cone, and its lower branches grow close to the ground. As it grows taller, its shape becomes rounder.

The lower branches of old trees are far above the ground, and their tops are often dead.

*Visitors standing beside the General Sherman Tree, believed to be the oldest and largest of all trees.*

One reason for the long life of the Big Trees is their thick, spongy bark. In older trees, this bark is often from ten inches to two feet thick near the base of the trunk. It is difficult for insects to get through the bark, or for fire to burn through it to the living sapwood.

All of the older sequoias have lived through many forest fires, and most of them bear fire scars hundreds of years old. These were caused by very hot fires that burned for days, or by several such fires.

Sometimes fire reached the heartwood and hollowed out the

6

*The base of the Uncle Ned Tree, showing the thick bark. The Visitor Center at Giant Forest is at the left.*

lower part of the tree. But if even a small amount of living sapwood is left, the tree continues to live and bear green foliage. Examples of such trees are the Room Tree and the Chimney Tree in Sequoia National Park.

The bark of the sequoia seems to have a healing quality. Almost as soon as a wound is made in a tree, the bark starts slowly to cover it. In the course of centuries, even the largest scars may be healed.

Very few sequoias die unless something causes them to fall. The Big Tree does not have a tap root.

Instead, it has many small roots that go out in all directions for a hundred feet or more. The roots are close to the surface of the ground. If the soil wears away from around the roots, the tree may become top-heavy and come crashing down.

Sequoia wood is very hard and does not decay readily. In the parks are huge trunks of fallen sequoias that have lain there for hundreds of years and are still in excellent condition. The Tunnel Log fell across the road and was so large that it could not be moved. So a tunnel was made through it.

*Union Pacific Railroad*

*The Tunnel Log on the road to Crescent Meadow.*

Giant Forest has the greatest number of Big Trees. It also contains the village, lodge and other overnight accommodations, and several well-kept campgrounds.

The Sentinel Tree towers over Giant Forest Village. Just across the road is Camp Kaweah, where the cabins have outdoor kitchens. Squirrels and chipmunks and tiny lizards play on nearby Beetle Rock.

Before starting a tour of Giant Forest, stop at the park museum, near the village, for a map and other information. The map shows that the General Sherman Tree is on the Generals Highway, two miles north of the village. Starting at this tree, a two-mile trail leads to the Congress Group, the Founders Grove, the Room Tree, and others. Visitors walking among these trees often say they feel as if they are in a great cathedral.

*Giant Forest Village and the Sentinel Tree.*

*Hubert Lowman*

*The Watchtower in Tokopah Valley, near Giant Forest. Tokopah is an Indian word meaning "high up."*

Near the General Sherman Tree, a side road turns off of the Generals Highway to Wolverton Corrals, where horses may be rented for trips into the high country. Nearby is Wolverton Pond, where only boys and girls up to twelve years of age may fish.

The five-mile trip to Heather Lake starts here. This trail goes by way of the Watchtower, a 1,000-foot cliff that looks down on beautiful Tokopah Valley. Aster, Emerald, and Pear lakes lie beyond Heather Lake.

An easier, two-mile trail starts at Lodgepole Camp and leads to the upper end of Tokopah Valley and Tokopah Falls. This trail goes along the foot of the Watchtower.

*Tokopah Falls cascade down the rocky cliffs from the lakes above, to form Marble Fork of the Kaweah River.*

*Hubert Lowman*

9

*The high peaks of the Great Western Divide, covered with snow most of the year.*

Starting again at Giant Forest Village, a three-mile road goes to Crescent Meadow. Alongside the road is the Auto Log, a huge fallen sequoia on which a road has been built. Cars can be driven over it with safety and ease.

Farther on, a side road turns off to Moro Rock. A 300-foot stairway, cut into the solid rock, goes to the top of this granite dome. From here there is a fine view of the lofty mountain range known as the Great Western Divide. These snowy peaks run through the central part of the park in a north and south direction.

Back on the main road, visitors pass the Parker group of Big Trees and drive through the Tunnel Log. They also pass the Black Chamber Tree, which was hollowed out by fire hundreds of years ago, but still continues to live and to produce new growth.

Many kinds of wildflowers bloom in lovely Crescent Meadow, and deer often feed here. A short trail leads to Log Meadow and Tharp's Cabin, built in a hollow fallen sequoia. Hale Tharp discovered the Big Trees in 1858. He was the first white man to see Giant Forest. For thirty summers he lived in this hollow log and pastured his cows in Log Meadow.

The High Sierra Trail, for hikers and horseback riders, starts at Crescent Meadow and goes into Sequoia's vast wilderness area. This famous trail crosses the Great Western Divide and ends at the top of Mount Whitney, at the east edge of the park. Mount Whitney was the highest mountain in the United States until Alaska, which has several higher peaks, became a state.

*Southern Pacific Railroad*

*Hikers in Sequoia's high country enjoy magnificent scenery.*

*Crystal Cave is the largest and most beautiful of the caves in the park.*

To explore lovely little Crystal Cave, visitors take a nine-mile drive from Giant Forest Village and then hike a half-mile down to the cave. Crystal Cave, which is lighted, was cut in white marble by an underground stream. This stream can be seen in places along the trail, as it flows through a channel of banded marble.

There are many beautiful and strange formations in the various rooms of the cave. Flowstone that looks like draperies hangs from the ceiling of the Curtain Room. In other rooms are great domes, glittering frostlike crystals, and formations that resemble icicles, huge slices of bacon, and a giant pipe organ.

12

Kings Canyon is about 65 miles from Giant Forest Village. After passing through the Lost Grove of Big Trees, the Generals Highway leaves Sequoia National Park. Soon it enters Grant Grove, in Kings Canyon National Park.

The high point of interest in this grove of Big Trees is the General Grant Tree. Nearby are the Tennessee, California, and General Lee trees.

A pioneer named Gamlin built the first cabin in Grant Grove, and this cabin is still standing. Before building it, he lived in the Fallen Monarch, a huge sequoia log that was hollowed out by fire. Later, this log served as a stable for thirty horses.

After leaving the Grant Grove section of the park, the road goes for 28 miles through Sequoia National Forest and along the South Fork of the Kings River. Then it re-enters Kings Canyon National Park at Cedar Grove.

*The famous General Grant Tree, in Grant Grove, is called the Nation's Christmas Tree. It is also a shrine for all the nation's war dead.*

13

Beyond Cedar Grove, the road goes along the bottom of Kings Canyon for six miles, through some of the finest scenery in the park.

*A modern highway follows the beautiful Kings River through spectacular scenery.*

*Kings Gate, along the Kings River Canyon Highway.*

Solid granite walls tower thousands of feet above us; the guide points out North Dome and Sentinel Dome. We pass Roaring River Falls and Zumwalt Meadow.

The road ends at Copper Creek, and trails fan out from here to the park's high country. They go to trout streams and high mountain lakes and meadows, which can be reached only by hikers or horseback riders.

Kings Canyon National Park has plenty of fine campgrounds, and there are overnight accommodations at Grant Grove and Cedar Grove.

*A view of North Dome.*

*A view of the valley from Inspiration Point, high above the Wawona Tunnel parking area.*

# Yosemite National Park

People come from all over the country to visit beautiful Yosemite, the third national park in California's great Sierra Nevada.

Yosemite Valley, which is seven miles long, a mile wide, and more than a half a mile deep, is famous for its magnificent scenery. Sheer granite cliffs and domes line the valley on both sides, and numerous waterfalls cascade down the walls in spring and early summer. Deer roam the woods and the wildflower meadows.

One of the best views of the valley is from the mouth of the Wawona Tunnel. On the right are Bridalveil Fall and Cathedral Rocks, with Half Dome and the peak known as Clouds Rest in the distance. At the left is the huge granite rock called El Capitan.

Yosemite is famous for its waterfalls, among them Vernal Fall, Nevada Fall, Bridalveil Fall, and Ribbon Fall. Most spectacular of all is Yosemite Fall.

It is at its best in late spring, when the waters from melting snow on the mountains leap over the cliff with a roar that fills the valley. The total descent of Yosemite Falls is nearly half a mile.

Yosemite Valley is a famous example of the work of glaciers during the Ice Age. A glacier moved down the valley, changing the gently sloping sides into straight, sheer walls. The streams that flowed down the slopes were left hanging, and now form waterfalls. The glacier scraped and polished granite domes and cliffs along the way, and neatly sliced off part of Half Dome.

*The Merced River, with lofty Half Dome, one of the major attractions for visitors to Yosemite, in the background.*

*Union Pacific Railroad*

16

Santa Fe Railway

*Jeffrey Pine at sunset in Yosemite.*

Yosemite National Park is open to visitors all year round. Several roads enter the park. Those through the Arch Rock and South entrances are kept open through the winters, but the others are open only during the summer season.

Two roads enter the valley and go to Yosemite Village. The Wawona Road comes in from the south and turns east at the Wawona Tunnel, where there is a beautiful view of the valley. The El Portal Road follows the Merced River into the valley. The Big Oak Flat Road, which goes past two groves of giant sequoias, comes in north of the El Portal Road and joins it just before it enters the valley.

Tioga Road crosses the park in the high country, above Yosemite Valley. This road is narrow and twisting, but it has beautiful scenery. Many granite domes, mountain meadows, and lovely lakes can be seen from it.

*Half Dome is reflected in the quiet water of Mirror Lake, almost a mile below.*

*Sunshine filtering through the trees on 11-Mile Trail. In the distance is the peak called Clouds Rest.*

19

*On summer nights, the firefall from Glacier Point is an unforgettable sight.*

Paul Nesbit

Many of the park's activities are centered in the valley. Yosemite Lodge, Camp Curry, Ahwahnee Hotel, and other facilities and campgrounds are here. There are also hotels and campgrounds at various places above the valley.

A fine museum at park headquarters has exhibits that explain how the valley was formed. Other exhibits tell about the wildlife in the park and about the Indians that once lived here. Naturalists are on hand to answer questions.

Every evening during the summer season, visitors in the valley gather at the Ahwahnee Hotel and Camp Curry to watch the firefall from Glacier Point. A bonfire of red-fir bark from fallen trees is waiting on the Point. At nine o'clock the embers from it are pushed over the edge and form a red, glowing firefall as they stream down the rock wall to a wide ledge 1,000 feet below.

Yosemite was the first national park to have naturalist programs, and they are especially good here. The Happy Isles Nature Center is headquarters for the Junior Rangers, made up of young people 8 to 12 years of age.

*Mule deer roam at will in Yosemite National Park.*

The Grizzly Club is also aimed at providing fun for the boys and girls who visit Yosemite Valley. The members of both organizations go on nature hikes, have bonfire programs, and do many other things to help them learn about plants, animals, and rocks of Yosemite.

There are hundreds of different kinds of wildflowers in the park. One that attracts much attention is the brilliant red snow plant.

The animals in the park include deer, bears, ring-tailed cats, different kinds of squirrels, and many other animals typical of the Sierra Nevada area.

*The snow plant has no green leaves. In springtime it pushes up through decayed matter in certain western mountain forests.*

The Mariposa Grove of giant sequoias, largest in the park, contains the Grizzly Giant, which is 209 feet tall and more than 3,000 years old.

Here, also, are the Clothespin Tree, which was burned completely through to a height of 70 feet, and the famous Wawona Tree. A tunnel was cut through the Wawona Tree in the early days, before the area became a national park, so that stagecoaches could go through it.

Visitors can eat lunch on the patio of the Big Trees Lodge, under the sequoias. Nearby, an interesting museum is housed in a faithful reproduction of a pioneer log cabin.

A few miles from the grove, on the Wawona Road, the Wawona Pioneer Village preserves old buildings, tools, a covered bridge, and other early-settler exhibits.

Yosemite's "high country" is world famous. Hundreds of miles of trails go to mountain peaks and meadows, to lakes and trout streams.

Five High Sierra Camps have been located about ten miles apart on the 53-mile High Sierra Loop. We can take a six-day horseback trip on this trail, starting at Yosemite Village and stopping at a different camp each night. There will be plenty of time to hike and fish along the way, too.

One of the High Sierra Camps is at beautiful Tuolumne Meadows, on the Tioga Road, and there is also a lodge here. Across the park, a short dirt road turns off Tioga Road to a lodge at White Wolf.

*Paul Nesbit*

ESTIMATED AGE - 3800 YEARS
HEIGHT                           209.0'
GREATEST DIAMETER OF BASE        34.7'
MEAN DIAMETER OF BASE            27.6'
HEIGHT OF FIRST LARGE LIMB       95.4'
DIAMETER OF FIRST LARGE LIMB     6.0'

*The Grizzly Giant, in Yosemite's Mariposa Grove of giant sequoias.*

Yosemite Park & Curry Co.

At sunny Tuolomne Meadows, the altitude is 8,600 feet. This is one of the largest and most beautiful mountain meadows in the High Sierra. The meadow is covered with wild flowers in July and August.

*Paul Nesbit*

23

# Death Valley National Monument

This monument encloses a strange and beautiful area, different from any other part of our country. It is a deep, narrow valley, 140 miles long and four to sixteen miles wide, lying between the rugged Amargosa Range on the east and the towering Panamint Range on the west. Most of the monument is in southeastern California, but the northeast corner extends into Nevada.

There are rocks in the valley almost as old as the earth itself. Salt flats mark the bed of an ancient lake. Animals who lived millions of years ago left their tracks in mud that has now become solid rock.

Death Valley was named by emigrants who tried to cross it during the Gold Rush to California. Now it is a pleasant winter resort, with comfortable hotels and motels, fine roads, and many interesting things to see. These include sand dunes, deeply eroded badlands, weird salt deposits, abandoned borax works, and deserted ghost towns.

Dante's View affords a wide, sweeping vista of Death Valley and of the range on range of mountains

*Dante's View.*

beyond. You look down on Badwater, which at 280 feet below sea level, is the lowest spot in the Western Hemisphere.

In the north end of the valley

are the ancient Ubehebe Volcano Crater and the modern, ornate Scotty's Castle. The castle was built by Walter Scott, once a trick rider in Buffalo Bill's Wildwest Show.

*Ubehebe Crater.*

*Scotty's Castle.*

# Muir Woods
# National Monument

This monument preserves a beautiful stand of coastal redwoods near San Francisco. These trees are taller and more graceful than the giant sequoias, but their trunks are more slender. They grow only along the California coast north of Monterey and for a short distance into Oregon.

Muir Woods Monument is small, only 485 acres, and several foot trails traverse it. Raccoons and other small animals live here, and deer may sometimes be seen in the early morning or late evening. After winter rains have raised the water level, salmon and steelhead trout may be seen going up Redwood Creek to their spawning beds.

*A shady grove of coastal redwood trees in Muir Woods.*

*National Park Service*

*Redwood Creek.*

# Joshua Tree National Monument

*Paul Nesbit*

*The Joshua Tree is an overgrown member of the lily family.*

Joshua Tree Monument preserves a typical southern California desert. The Joshua tree is only one of many interesting desert plants seen there.

This weird plant belongs to the lily family. It sometimes reaches a height of 40 feet, and its creamy white blossoms appear in clusters on the ends of its upstretched branches.

It is believed that the Mormons gave the plant the name of "Joshua Tree," or the "praying plant," because of its outstretched "arms."

Desert wildflower displays begin in March at the lower monument elevations and last through June in the highest areas. Washington palms flourish in several oases. Desert bighorn sheep, mule deer, coyotes, cougars, desert tortoises, lizards, and other typical desert animals live in the monument.

# Hawaii's National Parks

Both of these national parks contain live volcanoes, lava flows, lava tubes, spatter cones, and other interesting volcanic formations.

Hawaii National Park, on the island of Hawaii, contains two live volcanoes, Mauna Loa and Kilauea. Lava flows from Mauna Loa occupy more than 2,000 square miles of the island, but only the summit crater of the volcano and part of the northeast slope are in the park.

Mauna Loa rises 13,680 feet above sea level, and its lava flow extends to the bottom of the ocean, 18,000 feet below sea level. This volcano erupts at frequent intervals, sometimes destroying villages in the path of its lava flows.

Inside the summit crater of the Kilauea Volcano, 4,000 feet above sea level, is the smaller Halemaumau Crater. The Kilauea Iki, or Little Kilauea, and several others are outside the Kilauea Crater.

On the east slope of Kilauea are tropical rain forests, with ferns as large as trees. On the west slope, the Kau Desert contains many weird volcanic formations. Ohelo berry bushes, once sacred to Pele, goddess of volcanoes, grow in the desert. Hawaiians threw the berries into the crater during eruptions.

Park headquarters, containing a fine museum, and Volcano House, with overnight accommodations, are on the northeast rim of Kilauea Crater. An auto road circles the crater.

28

*Wolfe Worldwide*

*The lava flow from erupting Mauna Loa moving down to the sea.*

*A tropical rain forest in Hawaii National Park, where ferns grow as high as trees.*

Most of the eruptions of Kilauea have been through the Halemaumau Crater. But Kilauea Iki, which had been quiet for 90 years, suddenly came to life in mid-November of 1959.

The eruption started with a chain of fiery fountains, which soon died down to one. This fountain played at frequent intervals and became larger and larger. When it finally died after five weeks it had reached a new record height of 1,900 feet. Thousands of sightseers rushed to the park to see the magnificent display, and scientists studied it to learn more about the earth's interior.

A second eruption began in January, 1960, this time on the southeast flank of the mountain. Its lava engulfed a village and about forty other homes before it reached the sea, two miles away.

Haleakala, a huge volcano on the island of Maui, rises more than 10,000 feet above sea level. Hale-

National Park Service

*A fiery fountain of lava rises 600 feet during the eruption of Kilauea Iki in December, 1959.*

*Haleakala is one of the largest volcanoes in the world.*

akala is an old volcano, with rare eruptions separated by perhaps hundreds of years of inactivity. It was last active about 200 years ago.

Once a part of Hawaii National Park, the area became a separate park, Haleakala National Park, on July 1, 1961.

A highway goes past Silversword Inn and park headquarters, and zigzags from one overlook to another on the west rim of the crater.

The famed silversword, found only in Hawaii, grows on the sides and in the crater of Haleakala. This plant is a rounded cluster of stiff, narrow leaves that look like frosted silver. The tall blossom stalk is covered by 100 or more tiny purplish flowers. The plant takes from seven to twenty years to bloom and then dies as soon as the seeds are formed.

Other interesting plants, many of which are found nowhere else, grow on the lower slopes of Haleakala.

31                *Silversword plants.*